IT'S YOUR
WEIRDNESS
THAT MAKES YOU
WONDERFUL

Published by Mango Publishing Group, a division of Mango Media Inc.

Layout & Cover Design: Elina Diaz

Mango is an active supporter of authors' rights to free speech and artistic expression in their books. The purpose of copyright is to encourage authors to produce exceptional works that enrich our culture and our open society.

Uploading or distributing photos, scans or any content from this book without prior permission is theft of the author's intellectual property. Please honor the author's work as you would your own. Thank you in advance for respecting our author's rights.

For permission requests, please contact the publisher at:
Mango Publishing Group
2850 S Douglas Road, 2nd Floor
Coral Gables, FL 33134 USA
info@mango.bz

For special orders, quantity sales, course adoptions and corporate sales, please email the publisher at sales@mango.bz. For trade and wholesale sales, please contact Ingram Publisher Services at customer.service@ingramcontent.com or +1.800.509.4887.

It's Your Weirdness that Makes Your Wonderful: A Self-Acceptance Prompt Journal

Library of Congress Cataloging-in-Publication number: Has been applied for.

ISBN: (print) 978-1-64250-063-9, (ebook) 978-1-64250-064-6
BISAC: SEL004000—SELF-HELP / Affirmations

Printed in the United States of America

IT'S YOUR
WEIRDNESS
THAT MAKES YOU
WONDERFUL

A SELF-ACCEPTANCE PROMPT JOURNAL

BY KATE ALLAN
AUTHOR OF *YOU CAN DO ALL THINGS*

mango

CORAL GABLES

Table of Contents

Introduction   6

Rules   8

Set An Intention   16

Getting to Know You   18

Who Am I?   23

Let's Get You Mentally Healthy   30

To Read Everyday   44

Your Values   46

Taking Care of Your Mental Wellbeing   54

Structuring Your Mind   64

Body Acceptance   100

Relationships   114

Finding Joy (Where You Can)   124

So, in Conclusion   138

Extra Worksheets   141

About the Author   159

Introduction:

Hi there. My name is Kate Allan, and I'm an artist who draws sparkly, colorful things and writes about brains being bad. I find it's easier to absorb helpful information or a kinder perspective from something like a sunrise rabbit or a rainbow unicorn.

What you have in your hands here is a prompt journal that I hope will not only make you feel better in the short term, with some fun exercises and whimsical visuals, but will also help you to argue your negative thoughts and see yourself with compassion.

Why am I qualified to help with this? Okay, so, there's this concept that I learned when I was young— the best mathematics teachers are NOT people who are intuitively skilled at mathematics. Which is the opposite of what you'd think, right? No, the BEST mathematics teachers are people who struggled themselves with math. This is because they don't expect their students to intuitively understand anything! They will have had similar, if not the same, struggles with the process. Because of this, they are more patient and understanding, not of the material, but of the journey and process of learning.

So, what does this have to do with anything? In this analogy, I am the Math teacher who had to learn everything the hard way. Although I may not have everything figured out, I have come a long way. For a long time I honestly thought of myself as worthless, a waste of space. There was a two-month span in my early twenties where I actively avoided looking in mirrors because I absolutely loathed myself. And now? Well, I'm not going to lie to you and tell you I have an iron-clad ego, because I know I don't. But I will tell you I can now look into mirrors just fine. I can catch the self-abusive thoughts before they take root. This is my justification for helping show you how to develop better self esteem and a healthier outlook on yourself. If I can find a way to become healthier, you can, too.

So, come along with me. I will show you how I went from a terrible self image to a fairly healthy one. Because we all have to start somewhere, even if it's from the garbage. Or maybe especially if it's from the garbage.

RULES

OKAY, RULES.

Yes, there are rules.
They're helpful rules,
not stupid ones!
AND there are only two.

RULE 1:

YOU ARE ALLOWED TO MESS UP THIS JOURNAL

SCRIBBLE + DOODLE

~~CROSS THINGS OUT~~ AND TRY AGAIN

I don't want any *perfection* nonsense going on in here. This journal will only help if **1.** You are honest, and **2.** You allow yourself to be MESSY.

Here, I'll start the mess myself!

PLEASE,

just, like, scribble all over
this (mostly) blank page.

DRAW THE TORNADO

COMPLETE THE CAT

CIRCLE the things you like,
CROSS OUT the things you dislike.

RULE 2:

This journal is

YOURS, and
YOURS ALONE.

You never have to show
it to anyone else EVER,
if you don't want to.

**ALLOW YOURSELF TO
DIG INTO THE
DARK STUFF**

Allow yourself
to be sad, angry, guilty—
whatever you
need to feel.
It's all good,
it's ALL useful for
getting yourself to a
healthier place.

We are going to look at all sides of ourselves, both

THE UGLY & THE PRETTY

and learn to be okay with ALL of it.

And you can only get there if you feel safe doing it.

Set an Intention

Alrighty, you've sat down with this journal for this long, so you may have decided it's worth your time. Thank you for that. Your vote of confidence is rather encouraging!

Please bear with me on this little part. I need you to do something: Set an intention for what you'd like to get out of this prompt journal.

For example,

"I'm just going to make it through this journal to see what the hype is about," or "I actively hate myself, and I want to stop," or "I put everyone else first, and I am need to be better to myself."

THERE IS NO WRONG ANSWER.

WRITE DOWN WHAT YOU HOPE TO GET OUT OF THIS JOURNAL HERE:

_____

_____

_____

_____

_____

Thank you!

Now, what was the purpose of that? I have found when I start a workbook, a class, or a therapy session, that I am most helped when I have a clear goal in mind. And the thing is, that goal doesn't even need to be fulfilled most of the time for me to feel like it was time well-spent—I just find when I start something from a thoughtful place and with purpose, I am more likely to have a good result.

GETTING TO KNOW YOU

I want to do something fun! Let's take a figurative snapshot of you, right at this moment.

So please, indulge me. I want you to draw a stick figure version of yourself next to mine:

Hey, thanks.
We look great, don't we?

On to the interview!

1. What article of clothing do you feel cutest in? What clothes help you feel confident?

_____
_____
_____
_____
_____

2. How do you relax after a hard day?

_____
_____
_____
_____
_____

3. Can you recall the last time you changed an opinion? What was it about?

_____
_____
_____

changed opinion continued:

_____

_____

_____

4. What are three events that made you who you are today? And I mean, good, bad-- what are the top three?

1. _____

_____

_____

2. _____

_____

_____

3. _____

_____

_____

5. What's the best piece of advice you've ever heard?

_____

_____

_____

6. When have you felt most alive?

_____

_____

_____

7. What's the best thing about you?

_____

_____

_____

8. If you didn't have to sleep, what would you do with your extra time?

_____

_____

_____

_____

_____

_____

_____

_____

9. Where's the farthest you've been from home?

_____

_____

_____

10. What could you give a long presentation on with no preparation?

_____

_____

_____

11. What hobby would you like to try if money were no issue?

_____

_____

_____

12. What do you think about answering these questions?

☐ IT'S FUN.

☐ I DON'T LIKE THIS SORT OF THING.

☐ I HAVE NO OPINION.

WHO AM I?

Obviously, this question can be answered in many ways. Most people offer up their work:

"I'm a lawyer"

"I'm a musician"

"I'm a stay-at-home mom"

And I mean, there is some legitimacy to this because we spend a LOT of our time at our job.

I, HOWEVER, WOULD LIKE TO DIG A LITTLE DEEPER

you are who you love

Three people I love:

1. _____

2. _____

3. _____

What I admire about them:

1. _____

_____

_____

_____

_____

2. _____

_____

_____

_____

3. _____

_____

_____

_____

_____

you are your style

Three possessions that matter to me:

1. _____

_____

2. _____

_____

3. _____

_____

My favorite home decorations are:

_____

_____

_____

_____

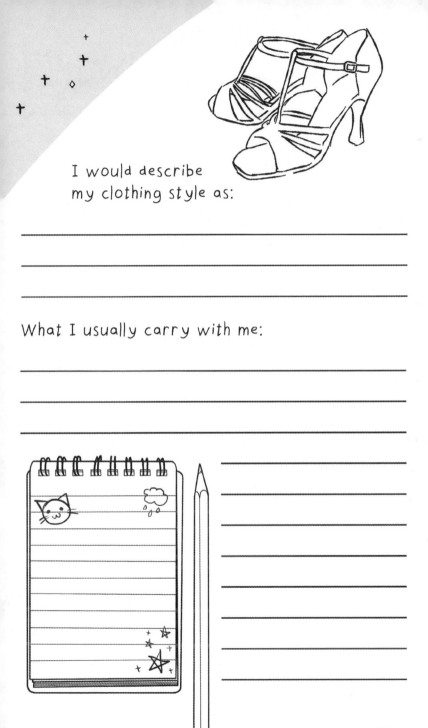

I would describe
my clothing style as:

_____

_____

_____

What I usually carry with me:

_____

_____

_____

you are what you like

I am a fan of...

this TV show:
_____

this book:
_____

this band:
_____

this comedian:
_____

_____

My hobbies are:

_____

_____

_____

_____

you are what you KNOW

I have studied:

_____

_____

_____

_____

I am pretty good at:

_____

_____

_____

_____

_____

_____

_____

The first step I took from the figurative self-image garbage can to getting myself into a healthier headspace was adopting mindfulness into my life.

mindfulness

So what is it? I define mindfulness as an awareness of your thoughts and emotions as well as an effort to stay present in the current moment.

STEP 1: NOTICE

What is one thing you feel? Give it a title—no worries about accuracy, just give it a guess.

STEP 2: OBSERVE

Where does the feeling show up in your body?

Is it pleasant, un|peasant, or neutral?

Observe for as long as you want.

STEP 3: SIT

Now, try your best to accept the feeling, no matter what it is, even if it's UGLY or UNFAIR.

Let go of judgement and sit with it.

SIT.

IMPORTANT: DO NOT IDENTIFY WITH THE FEELING

i.e. I am not <u>sad</u>, I am <u>experiencing sadness</u>.

TEMPORARY VISITOR

"YOUR EMOTION ≠ YOU"
—Debra E. Burdick

STEP 4: THINK IT THROUGH

What's the story behind this emotion, what thought triggered it?

When has this emotion showed up before?

Asking these questions will help you notice patterns and spiraling thoughts.

Please try this mindfulness exercise for yourself:

First, become aware of an emotion you're currently feeling.

Circle any of the emotions you feel.

Second, name what emotion you think it is, but don't worry too much about accuracy:

_____

Third, ask yourself: where does the emotion show up in my body?

_____

_____

Is the sensation pleasant, unpleasant, or neutral?

_____

Fourth, accept the emotion without judgement.

Important:
Do not identify with the emotion; it is NOT YOU.

TEMPORARY VISITOR

Now, breathe deeply, relax your muscles, get more comfortable.

Fifth, what is the story behind this emotion? What do you think triggered it?:

_____

_____

_____

_____

_____

_____

What do you usually do to cope with overwhelming emotions?

_____

_____

_____

_____

_____

_____

_____

_____

_____

Do you ever identify with your emotions? How do you feel about mentally distancing yourself from them?

_____

_____

_____

_____

_____

_____

_____

Do you think this mindfulness
exercise might be useful for you?
Why or why not?

_____

_____

_____

_____

_____

_____

_____

The second part of mindfulness that helped me (and this has some overlap with Cognitive Behavioral Therapy), is learning self-soothing.

Self-Soothing

First, it's important to note that ALL emotions serve a purpose.

Disgust: Can keep us from protracting illness or from accepting actions that may harm our social group

Anger: Can protect us from injustice or being taken advantage of

Fear: Prompts us to flee from danger

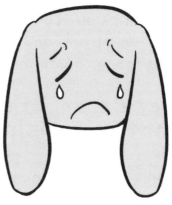

Sadness: Can generate a resolve to change and also validates loss

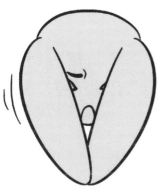

Shame: Can help prevent us from being socially ostracized

Embarrassment: Demonstrates self-awareness to our social group

In almost every case, your brain generates negative emotions because

IT'S TRYING TO PROTECT YOU.

So, knowing this, how can we handle our emotions and keep them from moving in permanently?

Here's an exercise that may help:

Think of your negative emotions like an overwhelmed, concerned little friend.

What are they trying to tell you?

What are they hoping to protect you from?

Now, if you can, try to:

ACKNOWLEDGE the concern,

REMEMBER your friend is doing its best to protect you, and

AFFIRM that things will be okay.

EMOTION BUDDY:
THEY HURT YOU, HURT THEM BACK

They DID hurt me, they must be having a really bad day. I'll be okay, though.

EMOTION BUDDY:
DON'T GO, YOU'RE GOING TO GET HURT

It may be dangerous, but I'll be okay. I can handle whatever happens.

Now, you try.

What would you say to the emotion buddy when they're freaking out?

I MESSED UP, I'M BAD

_____

_____

_____

_____

_____

_____

I LOOKED DUMB, NO ONE WILL LIKE ME

I WILL NEVER DO IT RIGHT!

WELL DONE!

As you learn to recognize and soothe your own worries, negative emotions will hijack your life less and less.

TO READ EVERY DAY:

1. You are NOT a burden on your loved ones.

2. YOU care TOO MUCH about what other people think.

3. THINGS ARE NEVER AS HOPELESS AS THEY SEEM.

4. ANY PROGRESS IS PROGRESS AND SHOULD BE CELEBRATED.

5. Please treat yourself nicely today.

YOUR VALUES

Your values may be the BIGGEST part of what makes you YOU. So, let's figure out what you value, shall we?

Please rate each category on a scale of 0 to 10:

0 being, "I don't care about this at all."
10 being, "This is VERY important to me."

Family (Other than your partner or your children):

0 1 2 3 4 5 6 7 8 9 10

Romantic Relationships:

0 1 2 3 4 5 6 7 8 9 10

Parenting:

0 1 2 3 4 5 6 7 8 9 10

Friendships and Social Life:
0 1 2 3 4 5 6 7 8 9 10

Work:
0 1 2 3 4 5 6 7 8 9 10

Education:
0 1 2 3 4 5 6 7 8 9 10

Self-Care (Food, Exercise, Sleep, Relaxation, etc.):
0 1 2 3 4 5 6 7 8 9 10

Community:
0 1 2 3 4 5 6 7 8 9 10

Fun:
0 1 2 3 4 5 6 7 8 9 10

Okay, so, EVERYTHING you rated 5 or above is QUITE IMPORTANT to you!

Values you rated 5 or more:

_____

_____

_____

_____

_____

Pro tip (yes, I am a pro): If you try and think of one thing you can do to honor each of your values, whether it's something you do once a month or once a day, you will FEEL more authentically yourself.

Acting on what you care about will help you feel more grounded and less pushed around by the world and events surrounding you.

Please, think, what are a few small things you can you can incorporate into your life that will honor your values?

A few examples:
 call my dad Saturday morning
 practice piano for 15 minutes Sunday night
 take a 20 minute walk every day

Ideas:

1. _____

_____

2. _____

_____

3. _____

_____

Taking time to remember what you value and then acting on those values will help you feel stronger;you will be more capable of taking on the world.

Note: Let growth come organically. You don't have to make every day an amazing milestone. Just grow here and there, showing improvement in small ways with every day you manage to finish.

Reflections:

Reflections:

TAKING CARE OF YOUR MENTAL WELLBEING

"Contentment is not being happy all of the time.
It is learning to cope with the hardships in between the bits of joy.
It is not taking the bits of joy for granted when they come.
And contentment is still possible even with a sick brain."
—the Frogman

STEP 1: BELIEVE IN GOOD

Whether that means in the universe, in humanity, or literally in your neighbor and your dog, please try to believe in the good in others.

THE GOOD I BELIEVE IN:

_____

_____

_____

_____

ACTIVELY

PRACTICE SELF-CARE

"Self love is asking yourself what you need—every day—and then making sure you receive it."
—Christine Arylo

Self love is something I've personally struggled with for a long time. How do we learn to feel admiration or even affection towards things we dislike about ourselves?

Well, I have since formed the opinion that it's more important to show ACTS of love towards ourselves rather than FEELINGS of

love. It's much easier to put myself in the frame of mind of a (reluctant) ally rather than an adoring fan.

So what is the most effective way to override self-loathing and take better care of ourselves?

Ask: "WHAT WOULD KID ME NEED TODAY?"

So, here's what I dpI make an effort to be cognizant of meeting my needs, and I do this by putting myself in the mind frame of taking care of a kid version of me.

"WHAT WOULD KID KATE NEED?"

Well, she needs ample time for sleep and rest, healthy food, fun and silliness, and mental transitions, like, "in 10 minutes I am going to go do this task." I've found my mental health has improved a LOT by doing this.

WHEN YOU CAN'T FIND LOVE FOR YOURSELF, TRY BEING YOUR OWN ALLY INSTEAD.

Please, if you wouldn't mind, rate your needs fulfillment for the last two weeks:

Sleep:

0 1 2 3 4 5 6 7 8 9 10

Eating nutritional food:

0 1 2 3 4 5 6 7 8 9 10

Drinking water:

0 1 2 3 4 5 6 7 8 9 10

General hygiene:

0 1 2 3 4 5 6 7 8 9 10

Fun:

0 1 2 3 4 5 6 7 8 9 10

Connecting with another person:

0 1 2 3 4 5 6 7 8 9 10

Taking prescribed medication:

0 1 2 3 4 5 6 7 8 9 10

Exercise:

0 1 2 3 4 5 6 7 8 9 10

Spending time outdoors:

0 1 2 3 4 5 6 7 8 9 10

I apologize if filling that out it is anything of an "oof" moment—it's not meant to shame you.

What would the child version of you need in the next two hours? Six hours?

_____

_____

_____

_____

_____

_____

Do you think actively taking care of "kid you" could help you meet your needs?

☐ It might.   ☐ I doubt it.

Self-care
the crap out of
life, and you'll get
through okay.

Do you find taking care of your needs to be stressful? If yes, why do you think that is?

_____

_____

_____

_____

_____

_____

Can you think of some small, actionable ways you can alter your day-to-day to make sure you better get what you need?

1. _____

_____

2. _____

_____

3. _____

_____

4. _____

_____

5. _____

_____

Time for another scribble page,
I think. Please, scribble away!

SET AN INTENTION
FOR YOUR DAY, WEEK, OR EVEN YOUR WHOLE LIFE

As stated earlier in this journal, I've found that moving through life with purpose helps me feel more in control. It means that when things go bad, I have a halfway formed plan of attack.

SOME INTENTIONS I HAVE FOUND USEFUL:

"Wherever I walk, everyone is a little bit safer because I am there.

Wherever I am, anyone in need has a friend.

Whenever I return home, everyone is happy I am there.

It's a better life!"

—Robert L Humphrey

"I have no idea how things
will get better, and I'm scared
out of my mind. Despite all of that,
I will keep fighting."

"I won't give up on myself,
no matter how hard it gets."

"I don't need a hero,
I can save myself."

Do any of these intentions
resonate with you?

Please, if you wouldn't mind, come up with
a couple possible intentions for yourself:

1. _____
_____
_____
_____

2. _____
_____
_____
_____

STRUCTURING YOUR MIND

You may think allowing your thoughts and self-abuse to fly around your mind willy-nilly is okay, but it's REALLY NOT. Like dogs and little kids, your mind NEEDS structure and discipline. When it steps out of line, it's imperative to your health that you be aware and ARGUE IT DOWN.

BAD FAT UGLY STUPID
INCOMPETENT
WASTE OF SPACE
WASTE OF TIME

Journaling

My goal with journaling is to understand my sometimes overwhelming negative feelings and predictions.
I structure this by first writing down the negative thought I'm struggling with, i.e.

"I'm gaining weight."

These negative thoughts tend to spiral to a dark place if I don't catch them.

For example:

"If I'm fat my boyfriend won't find me attractive.
   If I'm unattractive no one will love me.
      I will die alone."

This is obviously terrible for your health! So, what can be done?

What I find works best is similar to the concept of self-soothing, in that I need to analyze what assumptions I'm making, and then actively show kindness towards myself.

My assumptions:

1. That I am gaining weight.

2. That if I gain weight my boyfriend will find me unattractive.

3. That apparently no one is attracted to overweight women??

4. That apparently having extra fat makes a person unlovable???

5. That being unlovable means you'll die alone.

Try to picture what you'd respond if a friend said these assumptions to you. You'd probably tell them their ideas are totally off-base, and list all the evidence to the contrary. You'd let them know you think they're amazing, and their worries are unfounded. Well, though it can be difficult work, we need to be able to do that for ourselves.

Let's give it a try, shall we?

Assumption: I am gaining weight.

MY CHALLENGE TO THIS ASSUMPTION:
Weight fluctuates all the time, depending on your hormones and stress levels. It's also reasonable to drop the ball on your health for a while—life is difficult, and sometimes you need to focus on getting through rather than achieving all your goals. If you want to work on being healthier now, that's great, but make sure you're doing it for the right reasons.

Okay, would you like to give challenging a try? Please, think of what you'd say to a friend if they told you:

Assumption: If I gain weight my boyfriend won't be attracted to me anymore.

_____

_____

_____

_____

_____

_____

Assumption: I feel like when I'm overweight I'm unlovable.

_____

_____

_____

_____

_____

_____

_____

_____

_____

YOU CAN BE THE FRIEND YOU NEED

My final step is then asking myself, "what do you need to hear right now?" Or, "what can I tell myself that will calm these fears?"

I try to really dig in and get at the heart of the issue. In this case, the problem isn't actually my weight...

It's a fear that I will be undesirable, and thus unworthy of love and care.

Note: Getting to the heart of the issue can be difficult! In my case, it can take a lot of journaling, discussing fears with loved ones, and working through thought patterns with a therapist.

My kind response to this fear: you are lovable and worthy no matter what size you are.

Learning to argue with my thoughts like this and document subsequent affirmations has been one of the most fundamental parts of my mental health recovery.

A few kind responses to my fears that I have found helpful:

You are capable.

You can do this.

Whatever you manage to do today will be enough.

Those feelings
of inadequacy?
They're baseless.

You're doing
great.

You don't have
to be perfect to
be lovable.

How would you rate yourself on being aware of your assumptions?

0 1 2 3 4 5 6 7 8 9 10

Who do you typically open up to about your worries and fears?

_____

_____

_____

_____

Do you think it's possible to show kindness towards yourself, as if you were a friend?

☐ I can give it a try.

☐ No.

Why do you think it's so difficult for people to show kindness towards themselves?

_____

_____

_____

_____

_____

_____

_____

If you have difficulty showing kindness
and compassion towards YOURSELF, why
do you think that is?

_____

_____

_____

_____

_____

The only relationship
you're obligated
to stay in is
with yourself,
so you ought to start
treating
her right.

These next pages are for you to practice naming your assumptions and negative perceptions. Again, you never have to share this journal with anyone, so please do not feel worried about writing down your worries and fears. Journaling can help put them into a more realistic perspective—they lose some power when shared in a safe space.

And so you don't feel weird about it, I will start it off with some of my own fears/assumptions.

WHAT ARE YOU THINKING RIGHT NOW?

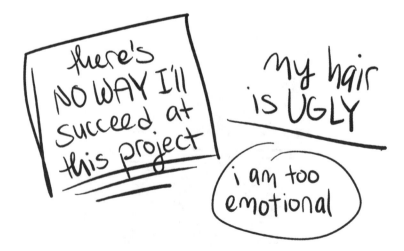

MY partner is tired of me

I AM TOO MUCH

I FEEL LIKE I AM A BURDEN

What kindness do you need to hear?

It's okay to fail! "The master has failed more times than the beginner has even tried." —Stephen McCranie

Everyone has bad hair days! It's no big deal. You're still cute, anyway.

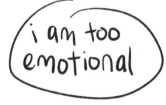

Nah, you're just tired and it makes things feel overwhelming.

Are you sure? He might just be busy and not engaging as much as usual.

And if he IS actually tired of you, that doesn't automatically mean you're tiring! Sometimes people just need space.

You're never "too much." You are lovable. You are worthy.

You are never a burden! You are doing your best with what you have, and it's enough.

WHAT ARE YOU THINKING RIGHT NOW?

_____

_____

_____

_____

_____

_____

_____

_____

_____

_____

_____

_____

_____

_____

_____

What kindness do you need to hear?

BANISH THE "SHOULDS"

One way in which I easily fall into mental self-abuse is feeling frustration over the things I "should" be doing, or not being the kind of person I "should" be. This comes from a place of shame rather than being properly motivating.

I have personally found this advice very helpful:

Instead of telling yourself, "I should get up," or "I should do this," ask yourself, "When will I get up?" or "When will I be ready to do this?"

"Instead of trying to order yourself to feel the signal to do something, which your brain is manifestly bad at, listen to yourself with compassionate curiosity and be ready to receive the signal to move when it comes."

—Tumblr user star-anise

Reflect: Do you ever feel like you "should" be different than you normally are? If yes, in what ways?

_____

_____

_____

_____

_____

_____

_____

_____

_____

_____

When I first heard this advice, I assumed asking myself, "When will I be ready?" would always result in a "never" answer. If you feel the same, will that worry prevent you from testing this technique?

☐ I will give it a try.

☐ I don't think this will work for me.

Own Your Time

A very helpful practice I learned in therapy was to assign my worries to a certain time of day, rather than having my thoughts overrun work, school, and relaxation time.

When it's time for work, focus on work. When it's time to relax, I need to be strict with myself mentally and fully experience that activity, whether it's a walk outside, a hot shower, or a tasty drink.

I've found I cannot fully get the rest I need if I'm either panicking or trying to solve work problems outside of work.

For a regular weekday, set your worry time and your relaxation time:

	:00	:15	:30	:45
6:00 AM				
7:00 AM				
8:00 AM				
9:00 AM				
10:00 AM				
11:00 AM				
12:00 PM				
1:00 PM				
2:00 PM				
3:00 PM				
4:00 PM				
5:00 PM				
6:00 PM				
7:00 PM				
8:00 PM				
9:00 PM				
10:00 PM				
11:00 PM				
12:00 AM				

Addressing Your Inner Critic

In contract law, "good faith" is a general assumption that all parties involved in the contract will deal honestly and fairly with each other. This means that in order for an agreement to be properly met, all parties need to show an amount of respect and sincerity towards each other.

So what does this have to do with us and our self-talk? Well, I argue that the only criticism we should apply to ourselves is in good faith. We need to provide PROPER constructive criticism, not just hate on ourselves when we mess up, or refuse to accept any fault at all.

Pointers on giving constructive criticism:

* The goal should be to better learn how to handle future problems, not shame yourself for mistakes.

* Focus on the SITUATION, not attributes of yourself.

* Offer concrete and actionable suggestions rather than vague ideas.

* Time it properly; only approach with criticism AFTER the event, when things have calmed down.

Note: the days you are feeling down or particularly negative are NOT the days where you should go into critique mode and try to address your problems. Odds are, your brain isn't working well enough to be properly fair towards itself.

ON BAD DAYS, IT'S BEST TO JUST FOCUS ON YOUR TASKS AND SURVIVE THE DAY.

If you're not feeling particularly critical of yourself today, please save this section for another time.

Reflect: In what ways were you critical of yourself today?

_____

_____

_____

_____

_____

_____

_____

_____

_____

_____

Do you that criticism came from a hope for growth or from a place of shame?

☐ hope for growth

☐ place of shame   ☐ not sure

If you're unsure, would you be comfortable critiquing a friend in this way? In other words, can you rephrase your criticism to be constructive and kind?

_____

_____

_____

_____

_____

_____

_____

_____

_____

_____

If there is no kinder way to phrase your criticism, it is time to send it to the mental trash can.

It is unfair and not worth your focus or energy.

If there IS a kinder way to phrase your criticism, what small, reasonable steps can you take forward?

_____

_____

_____

_____

_____

_____

_____

_____

_____

_____

If you can't take reasonable action, set that criticism aside. You have other things that are better worth your focus and energy right now.

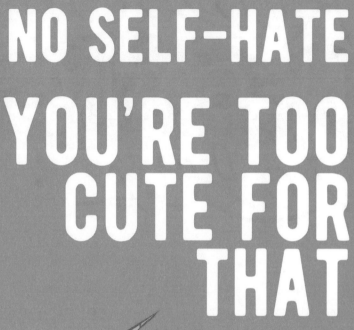

NO SELF-HATE YOU'RE TOO CUTE FOR THAT

Replacing NEGATIVE Labels

So, if you're anything like me, you may have ideas of yourself that are too harsh or not even accurate at all.

Some negative labels that have been applied to me throughout my life: lazy, cowardly, a burden, ungrateful, weird, ugly, mean, annoying, and overwhelming.

And honestly, I internalized a lot of those labels. I thought that in order to be acceptable to others, I needed to really take those judgements in and shape myself into the person they wanted me to be.

In order to not be seen as
COWARDLY, I hid all symptoms
of my anxiety and panicked alone.

In order to not be seen as
ANNOYING, I reworked my
personality to be less amiable
and more quiet.

In order to not be seen as LAZY,
I overworked myself trying to get
good grades and do more than my
bosses asked for.

In order to not be seen as
UGLY, I exercised too much
and didn't eat enough.

In order to not be OVERWHELMING,
I did not share my
true self with others
and was left unknown
and unseen.

Did any of these actions result in my better health or happiness? NO. I was so concerned with not having negative traits that I hurt myself in order to please others. And you know what? They weren't pleased, anyway!

"Cut myself into pieces
easy to chew
Carve me up into
someone you'd like to choose
Till I'm only pieces of you"

—Tessa Violet, "Words Ain't Enough"

TWO MAJOR PROBLEMS WITH INTERNALIZING NEGATIVE LABELS:

1. They are other people's judgements

2. It's bad-faith criticism—its aim is to shame/hurt rather than help

I would urge you to have another look at the negative traits that have been assigned to you. Is there more to the story?

When you were called lazy, were you actually resting or unsure about what to do next? When you were called annoying, were you in a good mood while the person you were talking to was in a bad one? When you were called weird, were you enjoying something someone else thought was childish or silly?

Try, if you can, to look at past you with curiosity and compassion.

What are negative labels that have been applied to you?

_____

_____

_____

_____

_____

_____

_____

_____

_____

_____

_____

_____

Do you think those negative labels are **100**% fair?

☐ No.

☐ Yes.

Okay, let's try to reframe them. If you look at your past self with compassion, are there kinder labels you could assign to yourself? For example: "I'm not lazy, I'm careful," or, "I'm not mean, I stick to my boundaries."

_____

_____

_____

_____

_____

_____

_____

_____

_____

_____

_____

In what ways does adopting negative labels serve you? Can you think of any ways they help you to be happier or healthier?

_____

_____

_____

_____

_____

_____

_____

Stop calling yourself garbage. You're a blueberry fairy princess, you're amazing.

Try to let go of what you can't control

Your best will look different than everyone else's. It just will. You came from different circumstances, you have a different brain.

Try to find compassion for your younger self amid all the pain and difficulty rather than disappointment and regret. There's no point in shaming yourself about your past when it's not something you can change. All we can do from this point, right now, is try to learn from our choices and their consequences.

Also, and I say this coming from my own experiences, starting from self shame is NEVER going to get you very far.

I belive the healthiest thing a person can do is accept themselves compassionately as they are, and then aim for the person they want to be.

"The curious paradox is that when I accept myself just as I am, then I can change."
—Carl R. Rogers

The truth is, YOU HAVE ALWAYS DONE THE BEST WITH WHAT YOU HAVE HAD.

I may not be who I want to be, but I'm not so bad, either.

Reflect: What do you think is holding you back from accepting yourself as you are right now? Are there things about you that you feel are unacceptable?

_____

_____

_____

_____

_____

_____

_____

_____

_____

_____

_____

_____

_____

_____

_____

_____

Try to look at it objectively: are you being 100% fair to yourself?

☐ Probably not.

☐ Yes.

Why do YOU think self-acceptance is difficult for so many people?

_____

_____

_____

_____

_____

_____

_____

_____

_____

_____

_____

_____

_____

_____

Body Acceptance

"The nitrogen in our DNA, the calcium in our teeth, the iron in our blood, the carbon in our apple pies were made in the interiors of collapsing stars.

We are made of star stuff."

—Carl Sagan

Draw stars inside the girl and the animals!

We feel a lot of pressure from society to look differently than we do naturally, don't we? In order to

be liked, impressive, get the guy,

keep the guy, get the job, be wanted, be admired, be loved, be lovable—we receive the message that we need

to be FLAWLESS.

I pinch my belly fat more than

I'd like to admit. I scowl at my body when it rolls or jiggles. I label myself as defective, undisciplined, gross,

and low in value.

Lots of us have been here, right? And we go through some similar observations; "I am more cruel to myself than others. I see other bodies as beautiful. I do not focus on others' flaws, or I do not even see them as having flaws."

Let's try to look at our bodies in another way.

As tempting as it may be, you can't **HATE YOURSELF** into **HEALTH**

Your body does AMAZING things just to exist. Your body does so much, constantly, just to take care of you. It is always working, without you thinking about it.

STUFF YOUR BODY DOES ALL THE TIME WITHOUT YOU TELLING IT TO

Takes around
20,000 breaths DAILY

Processes about
50 gallons of blood DAILY

Heart beats around
100,000 times DAILY

Repeat after me:

MY BODY IS AMAZING

IT TAKES
CARE OF ME

IT PROTECTS ME

IT ENABLES ME
TO EXPERIENCE
WONDERFUL THINGS

Okay, so we can objectively say bodies are amazing, right? They take care of many things without our conscious directive. So, how can I try to get a handle on the disgust I feel towards myself?

PLEASE, CONTINUE TO REPEAT AFTER ME:

I DON'T OWE ANYONE A BEAUTIFUL BODY.

I DON'T OWE ANYONE A FLAT STOMACH.

I DON'T OWE ANYONE
SMOOTH SKIN.

I DON'T OWE ANYONE
TONED MUSCLES.

I DON'T OWE ANYONE
AN ATTRACTIVE FACE.

I DON'T OWE ANYONE
A HAIRLESS BODY.

THERE IS NO HEALTHY
PLACE FOR SELF-DISGUST.

EMBRACE THE
IMPERFECTION.

feeling pretty AND pimply

feeling fat AND fabulous

feeling bloated AND beautiful

One more thing, I got this as
a tip from a follower on Instagram,
and it has really helped reset my
perspective; if you think something
unkind towards yourself,

APOLOGIZE FOR IT.

Your body is doing a great job.
It doesn't deserve cruelty.

i know it can be hard
to see for yourself, so take
it from a rainbow T-rex:

**you're actually
pretty f***ing great**

Reflections:

Reflections:

relationships

"When exercising empathy it's important to remember you can't carry someone's burdens for them. They still have to do the work."

—@SharpSweetBella on Twitter

WHAT ARE HEALTHY WAYS OF CARING FOR SOMEONE?

 BEING A LISTENER, VALIDATING FEELINGS WHEN APPROPRIATE (you should not do this for your parents or boss, for example),

AND CHOOSING TO DO SMALL ACTS OF KINDNESS ("Can I get you some tea?") are all healthy ways of caring for someone.

Okay, let's cover some important ground here: your rights as a person.

YOUR RIGHTS

1. You have the right to say "no" to any demand or request.

2. You have the right to protest treatment that is cruel or unfair.

3. You have the right to feel and express your emotions and your pain, even though they may be distasteful to others.

4. You have the right to your opinions, goals, ideals, and convictions.

5. You have the right to ask for help and support from others, though you may not always receive it.

6. You have the right to be the final judge of your morals and beliefs.

Repeat after me:

I DO NOT HAVE TO JUSTIFY MY ACTIONS TO EVERY PERSON.

I DON'T OWE FRIENDSHIP OR ROMANTIC AFFECTION TO ANYONE.

I AM NOT RESPONSIBLE
FOR ANYONE ELSE'S
PROBLEMS.

I AM NOT RESPONSIBLE
FOR ANYONE ELSE'S
HAPPINESS.

What does any of this have to do with self-acceptance? Well, in my experience, my relationships have had a HUGE impact on how I've viewed myself.

The healthiest relationships have good, sturdy boundaries. The most understandable definition I've found of boundaries is this:

> "A clean, clear boundary preserves your individuality, your YOUNESS. You are an individual, set apart, different, unique. Your history, experiences, personality, interests, dislikes, preferences, perceptions, values, priorities, skills—this unique combination defines you as seperate from others."
> —Anne Katherine

I have had to learn the hard way that when I take on others' responsibilities, or change a fundamental part of myself for someone else, I deny myself true intimacy. It's not possible to be truly known (which we all crave as human beings) if my boundaries are not upheld.

I have found the best way to develop healthy boundaries is to learn who I am and try my best to take care of that person. In order to be healthy, we have to actively advocate for ourselves. And honestly? Not everyone is okay with us doing that.

Characteristics of a Healthy Relationship:

1. Boundaries: Each person in the relationship is clear and seperate from one another, allowed their own interests, preferences, and values

2. Communication: Each person in the relationship feels safe and welcome to share their true feelings and opinions

3. Trust: Each person in the relationship knows they can rely on the other, there is no fear of harm from the other

4. Consent: Each person in the realtionship continually gives their "okay" on how events proceed

Do you currently feel responsible for someone else's happiness or problems? If so, how does it make you feel?

_____

_____

_____

_____

_____

_____

_____

_____

_____

_____

_____

_____

_____

_____

_____

_____

_____

_____

_____

Do you fear setting boundaries with others? If so, why do you think that is?

_____

_____

_____

_____

_____

_____

_____

_____

_____

_____

_____

_____

_____

_____

_____

_____

_____

_____

_____

You don't have to settle for anyone who treats you poorly. There are people in the world who will treat you with kindness and respect, you just need patience in finding them.

And you will always have YOU.

You're capable, strong, and resilient, even when you feel like you're not.

YOU ARE NOT AN ENDLESS FOUNTAIN OF ENERGY AND GOODNESS.

DO NOT SACRIFICE YOUR WELLBEING FOR OTHER PEOPLE.

Finding Joy (where you can)

> "We should avoid fixating on a specific happiness level and recognize that happiness itself is not a goal but a fleeting by-product of progress towards other goals."
> —Jon Rottenburg

CELEBRATING SMALL VICTORIES

Something that always felt a little silly to me was celebrating small victories, but once you start, it can become very addicting.

If you can, try to at least acknowledge to yourself every time you've accomplished something that was difficult for you.

Victories I personally make a note to celebrate are: making it to the top of each hill while exercising, finishing every stage of an illustration, and sometimes even just getting out of bed.

PLEASE, LIST SOME SMALL VICTORIES YOU ACCOMPLISHED TODAY:

1. _____

2. _____

3. _____

4. _____

5. _____

GOOD JOB TODAY!

I LOVE YOU!

I'M A KITTEN!

REALIZE YOU'VE HANDLED A LOT

"Courage doesn't always roar.
Sometimes courage is the little voice
at the end of the day that says
I'll try again tomorrow."
—Mary Anne Radmacher

Life really can feel overwhelming
sometimes. If your mind is anything like
mine, it predicts that THIS day will be
the one that I can't handle. But, honestly,
I have a pretty good track record, and
I bet you do, too.

Look at
everything you
have survived so
far. You weren't
defeated then,
you won't be
defeated now.

I CURRENTLY HAVE
A CONSECUTIVE
11,000
DAYS HANDLED.

HOW MANY
DO YOU HAVE?
(365 X YOUR AGE)

THIS IS AWESOME.

Thanks for
sticking it out,
honestly.

PLEASE, LIST SOME SMALL VICTORIES YOU ACCOMPLISHED TODAY:

1. _____

_____

2. _____

_____

3. _____

_____

4. _____

_____

5. _____

_____

_____

You don't have to maximize the potential of every day.

PLEASE, LIST SOME SMALL VICTORIES YOU ACCOMPLISHED TODAY:

1. _____

_____

2. _____

_____

3. _____

_____

4. _____

_____

5. _____

_____

Some days are just about getting through.

TREAT YOURSELF

Another way to keep the daily positive brain chemicals flowing is to reward yourself for getting through the day. Life is rarely easy, and the things you find difficult are absolutely valid. The best way to legitimize those efforts is to show yourself some self-care at the end of the day.

Some ways I treat myself:

* Watching terrible '80s movies

* Drinking tea and reading

* Taking a short walk to look for flowers, birds, or cats

* EXFOLIATING ALL MY SKIN using a salt or sugar scrub

* Lighting candles or twinkle lights

* Hanging up artwork

Please, name a few ways you can regularly treat yourself for getting through your day:

1. _____

2. _____

3. _____

4. _____

5. _____

EMBRACE YOUR WEIRD

I love those who freely enjoy themselves without fear of ridicule—people who dance when there's a live band playing, people who collect antique toys, and people who dress dappered up in all pastels.

Do you think I would be making my artwork if I didn't heartily embrace my weird? I can't tell you how many negative comments I've gotten—there are many people who think it's silly, stupid, embarassing, and pointless.

I've come to realize that just because there are a few people who think I'm a weirdo, that shouldn't keep me from enjoying what I love. Creating colorful artwork and writing about mental health brings me joy.

The fact is, your favorite actress has unabashed haters. Your favorite book has 1-star reviews. Do those creators let that stop them from doing what they love?

you don't need to be appealing to everyone

Have you ever let go of something that brings you joy because of others? Have you put off trying a new look or hobby for fear of how others will react?

YOUR LIFE IS FOR YOU. Please, take a moment to commit that to yourself. Please allow yourself every joy possible that you can find.

Please, repeat after me,
MY LIFE IS FOR ME.

Reflections:

Reflections:

So, in conclusion:

Well, in my estimation, you've gone through this prompt journal because you hope things can get better—you wouldn't bother if you thought self-acceptance was a crock of hooey. And honestly, believing things can improve is the BIGGEST step towards being healthy. If you're paying attention to what hurts and what helps, you will naturally improve your life. You're a smart cookie.

The truth is, lots of people do not try to grow or help themselves. Many people live their entire lives being battered by their emotions and only dealing with what's right in front of them. You? You're trying things. You're not letting pain or fear get in the way of what you want for yourself. That is unusual. That is admirable. That is badass.

I hope you feel somewhat validated and feel a little more motivated to keep trying. I certainly want you to.

All My Love,
Kate

HEY.
YOU MATTER.
THANKS FOR
EXISTING.

Extra Worksheets

Please try this mindfulness exercise for yourself:

First, become aware of an emotion you're currently feeling.

Circle any of the emotions you feel.

Second, name what emotion you think it is, but don't worry too much about accuracy:

_____

Third, ask yourself: where does the emotion show up in my body?

_____

_____

Is the sensation pleasant, unpleasant, or neutral?

_____

Fourth, accept the emotion without judgement.

Important:
Do not identify with the emotion; it is NOT YOU.

TEMPORARY VISITOR

Now, breathe deeply, relax your muscles, get more comfortable.

Fifth, what is the story behind this emotion? What do you think triggered it?:

_____

_____

_____

_____

_____

_____

Please try this mindfulness exercise for yourself:

First, become aware of an emotion you're currently feeling.

Circle any of the emotions you feel.

Second, name what emotion you think it is, but don't worry too much about accuracy:

_____

Third, ask yourself: where does the emotion show up in my body?

_____

_____

Is the sensation pleasant, unpleasant, or neutral?

_____

Fourth, accept the emotion without judgement.

Important:
Do not identify with the emotion; it is NOT YOU.

TEMPORARY VISITOR

Now, breathe deeply, relax your muscles, get more comfortable.

Fifth, what is the story behind this emotion? What do you think triggered it?:

_____

_____

_____

_____

_____

_____

WHAT ARE YOU THINKING RIGHT NOW?

_____

_____

_____

_____

_____

_____

_____

_____

_____

_____

_____

_____

_____

_____

_____

_____

_____

What kindness do you need to hear?

_____

_____

_____

_____

_____

_____

_____

_____

_____

_____

_____

_____

_____

_____

WHAT ARE YOU
THINKING RIGHT NOW?

_____

_____

_____

_____

_____

_____

_____

_____

_____

_____

_____

_____

_____

_____

_____

_____

What kindness do you need to hear?

_____

_____

_____

_____

_____

_____

_____

_____

_____

_____

_____

_____

_____

_____

PLEASE, LIST SOME SMALL VICTORIES YOU ACCOMPLISHED TODAY:

1. _____

2. _____

3. _____

4. _____

5. _____

You don't have to maximize the potential of every day.

PLEASE, LIST SOME SMALL VICTORIES YOU ACCOMPLISHED TODAY:

1. _____

_____

2. _____

_____

3. _____

_____

4. _____

_____

5. _____

_____

Some days are just about getting through.

PLEASE, LIST SOME SMALL VICTORIES YOU ACCOMPLISHED TODAY:

1. _____

2. _____

3. _____

4. _____

5. _____

You don't have to maximize the potential of every day.

PLEASE, LIST SOME SMALL VICTORIES YOU ACCOMPLISHED TODAY:

1. _____

2. _____

3. _____

4. _____

5. _____

Some days are just about getting through.

Reflections:

Reflections:

_____
_____
_____
_____
_____
_____
_____
_____
_____
_____
_____
_____
_____
_____
_____
_____
_____
_____
_____
_____
_____
_____
_____
_____
_____
_____
_____
_____
_____

About the Author

Kate Allan is an author, artist, and the creator of the mental health art blog, *The Latest Kate*. A Southern California transplant, she enjoys anything bright, fluffy, or colorful, as can be seen in her work. When she isn't endeavoring to soak up every ray of sunshine, she works as a freelance designer and illustrator.

Her first book is *You Can Do All Things: Drawings, Affirmations, and Mindfulness to Help with Anxiety and Depression*.

Twitter: @tlkateart
Instagram: @thelatestkate
Blog: thelatestkate.tumblr.com
FB: facebook.com/thelatestkate

Mango Publishing, established in 2014, publishes an eclectic list of books by diverse authors—both new and established voices—on topics ranging from business, personal growth, women's empowerment, LGBTQ studies, health, and spirituality to history, popular culture, time management, decluttering, lifestyle, mental wellness, aging, and sustainable living. We were recently named 2019's #1 fastest growing independent publisher by *Publishers Weekly*. Our success is driven by our main goal, which is to publish high quality books that will entertain readers as well as make a positive difference in their lives.

Our readers are our most important resource; we value your input, suggestions, and ideas. We'd love to hear from you— after all, we are publishing books for you!

Please stay in touch with us and follow us at:

Facebook: Mango Publishing
Twitter: @MangoPublishing
Instagram: @MangoPublishing
LinkedIn: Mango Publishing
Pinterest: Mango Publishing

Sign up for our newsletter at www.mango.bz and receive a free book!

Join us on Mango's journey to reinvent publishing, one book at a time.